GIFTED & TALENTED Pocketbook

By Barry
Hymer

Cartoons:
Phil Hailstone

Published by:

Teachers' Pocketbooks
Laurel House, Station Approach,
Alresford, Hampshire SO24 9JH, UK
Tel: +44 (0)1962 735573
Fax: +44 (0)1962 733637
E-mail: sales@teacherspocketbooks.co.uk
Website: www.teacherspocketbooks.co.uk

*Teachers' Pocketbooks is an imprint of
Management Pocketbooks Ltd.*

Series editor – Linda Edge.

© Barry Hymer 2009.

This edition published 2009.
Reprinted 2010, 2012, 2013.

ISBN 978 1 906610 01 2

E-book ISBN 978 1 908284 89 1

British Library Cataloguing-in-Publication
Data – A catalogue record for this book is
available from the British Library.

Design, typesetting and graphics by **efex Ltd**.
Printed in UK.

Contents

Gifted & Talented Pocketbook

This is a wonderful book. It's fascinating, it's profound, and it's practical!

Carol Dweck,
Professor of Psychology, Stanford University.

A marvellously lucid and engaging introduction to the 21st century way of thinking about giftedness. Every G&T teacher should have a pocket for it!

Guy Claxton,
Professor of the Learning Sciences,
University of Winchester.

At last, a book on G&T that is inspiring! It's based in sound educational values and fundamental evidence about learning.

Chris Watkins,
Reader, London Institute of Education.

'We pass through this world but once. Few tragedies can be more extensive than the stunting of life, few injustices deeper than the denial of an opportunity to strive or even to hope, by a limit imposed from without but falsely identified as lying within.'

Stephen Jay Gould –
The Mismeasure of Man

Mystery or Mastery?

 Motivation – Intelligence's Motor

 Grow!

 Relate!

 Act!

 Challenge!

 Exert!

Mystery
or Mastery?

'Gifted and talented' – a recent history

It seemed so simple in the post-war years: 'bright' children were destined for grammar schools and professional careers, and the 'less able' were destined for secondary moderns and vocational futures in the trades. Comprehensives, in turn, aimed to service all abilities, and 'differentiation' was the buzzword. Whilst accusations flew to and fro about whether or not these systems were 'elitist and discriminatory' or 'failing to stretch the ablest,' the notion of 'ability' was rarely questioned. Few wondered whether the concept itself might need updating.

Towards the end of the 20th century the term 'gifted and talented' entered the formal vocabulary of English schools, first through the Excellence in Cities Programme and then through a welter of emerging national structures and 'G&T' initiatives. Many of these morphed into the 'personalised learning' and 'narrowing the gap' agendas, and now survive in inspectors' reports exhorting schools to increasing challenge for the more able.

Carpe diem – seize the day! We now have the opportunity to take G&T away from the mean streets and dead-ends of 'ability,' 'identification' and 'cohorts' and turn instead into the open avenues of learning and gift-creation for all.

G&T – a new look at a familiar concept

Whilst valuing and celebrating the many examples of best practice in G&T that have emerged over the past decade and more, this Pocketbook sets out a vision that diverges from familiar paths. It has arisen from years of experimentation with and exposure to different ways of thinking about this field of education, and from observing outstanding teachers at work with their students.

The *Gifted & Talented Pocketbook* is a response to the dissatisfactions that I and many teachers feel with the principles and outcomes that underpin the traditional, data-driven framework. That framework promotes a 'test-and-place' and 'them-distinct-from-the-rest-of-them' practice which can actually hinder the development of gifts and talents. This book offers a challenging, invigorating and realistic alternative, fit for the 21st century.

What remains is a commitment to ensuring that *all* pupils, including those already working at an advanced level, receive educational opportunities that allow them to be appropriately stretched, engaged and challenged.

Will this approach work for me?

You are likely to find much in this Pocketbook's approach to giftedness that
you can identify with if you subscribe to the following values, beliefs and principles:

- Children do not have the same skills and strengths, but all can respond well to
  rich, challenging, personalised educational opportunities
- Gifts and talents aren't 'found,' 'discovered' or 'identified' in children – they're
  made, created and grown
- Gifts and talents aren't stable, measurable attributes – they wax and
  wane along with children's educational environments, the quality of
  their relationships, their commitment and dedication, and other factors
- A focus on children's *performances* and on teacher-imposed targets
  is less likely to lead to a long-term passion for learning (and
  achievement) than a focus on their *learning*, and their
  personally-generated targets

*'The healthy functioning community depends on
realising the capacity to develop each [child's] gift.'*
Peter Senge (Society for Organizational Learning)

Who's gifted? Definition 1

So what exactly do we mean when we label someone as 'gifted' and how do we decide who is? Do we need to? There are hundreds of definitions of giftedness, but since labels lead our thinking as well as describe it, let's give some serious thought to a couple of these. First, a very familiar one:

> Exceptional academic ability or potential relative to one's peer group.

And a related way of 'reading' Safia, a Year 6 pupil:

> It's no wonder Safia's so bright. Her parents are both highly able people themselves. Her exceptional academic achievements are explained by her natural giftedness. She clearly needs special provision, and she has in fact responded well to the accelerated literacy and numeracy provision she's had access to as part of our school's G&T cohort. She's one of our success stories and is destined for great things.

Who's gifted? Definition 2

Now consider this less familiar definition of giftedness:

> A preparedness to invest time, energy and resources (intellectual, physical, emotional, social) into an area of learning.

And a related 'reading' of Safia:

> Safia has responded tremendously well to her stimulating and supportive home background and to the opportunities she's had in school. She's achieving wonderfully well but is showing signs of being more interested in her scores and class position than in her learning, and she's nervous of 'failure'. She seems, however, to have a genuine interest in art and design – how might I best help her to deepen and extend her interest in this area?

Which of these definitions and 'readings' do you hear most often in the staffroom? Which do you feel most comfortable with? Why?

Definitions – pros and cons

Definition 1 has one huge pro: it's comfortably familiar. It's so steeped in our national psyche that it barely needs stating. Some kids are just brighter than others. The very brightest are gifted. Period.

The problem with this norm-referenced definition? Despite the frequency of their use, no-one can claim definitively to know just what the terms 'brightness', 'ability', 'potential', 'intelligence', 'cleverness', 'giftedness', etc actually mean. We may *think* we know what they mean. They might share some family resemblances but they are tools, not essences. And whilst we might believe we can measure them through IQ tests and the like, we have no widely accepted understanding as to what exactly *them* is. In the words of the late Michael Howe, we have *'a measure in search of a concept'*.

Definition 2 has the big pro of being related to the learning of the individual, not to any comparison group. Moreover, it needs no big brother concept like *ability*, *potential* or *intelligence* to make sense of it. Its con? We can't easily measure it. And if that's the case, can it have value in our education system?

Definitions – some implications for you, the teacher

The two different definitions of 'giftedness' lead to contrasting responses to questions you might ask/be asked about Safia or any other child:

	1. 'Exceptional ability or potential'	2. 'An investment of time, energy and personal resources'
Who decides if Safia's gifted?	You do, based on her standardised test and attainment results and other norm-referenced performance measures.	You both do, based on her responses to rich, stimulating learning experiences provided over time and your careful observation of these.
What emphasis do I give to identification strategies?	A lot – these need to be comprehensive, detailed and accurate, as appropriate provision rests on the outcomes.	Precious little – identification is secondary to and a function of her responses to high-quality provision.

Further implications for you, the teacher

	1. 'Exceptional ability or potential'	2. 'An investment of time, energy and personal resources'
Do I need to label her as gifted?	Yes, why not? It provides a focus for intervention, corrects an imbalance in resources and helps her feel good about herself.	No, it distracts us all from the truly educational endeavour: to promote learning, not complacency. Giftedness is a fluid concept, not fixed.
What do I tell her parents?	That she's been designated gifted, the reason/s why, and what opportunities she can access now. What's there to hide? They have a right to know.	What personalised provision Safia is receiving, and how she's responding to it. Where she might be going next and what her parents can do to support this.
How much support can I expect in taking this approach with Safia and others?	Huge amounts: this is the predominant approach, beloved of many. It is relatively easy to administer, track and monitor, and will be familiar to parents, inspectors and national initiatives.	That depends: does your school value learning and child-led enquiry even more than short-term performance and hitting external targets? Can you communicate your rationale to parents and inspectors, and back it up?

Raising the bar

So which approach does this Pocketbook promote? Your powers of inferential reading have already answered this!

This book acknowledges its debt to traditional, orthodox understandings of 'giftedness,' yet invites you to raise the bar and to jump a little higher – in the belief that an approach which puts gift-creation above gift-identification will permit your students to think the impossible and thereby reach even higher levels.

It's the sort of mindset that in the 1968 Olympics encouraged Dick Fosbury to think differently, and in so doing to jump differently, turning a Flop into a Giant Leap.

Are gifts caught or taught?

'The great thing and the hard thing is to stick to things when you have outlived the first interest, and not yet got the second, which comes with a sort of mastery.' **Janet Erskine Stuart** (Educationalist)

The Canadian psychologist Prof Dona Matthews coined the terms **'mystery'** and **'mastery'** frameworks to discriminate between two ways of understanding giftedness:

1. Is it shrouded in *mystery*: no-one knows why; you just *are* gifted – maybe it's genetic, maybe it's luck – who knows?

Or

2. Is it something you can learn or *master* if you have the opportunity and the right attitude and are prepared to work hard?

Mystery vs mastery

	Mystery Framework	Mastery Framework
Are gifts and talents caught or taught?	Largely caught.	Largely taught.
Emphasis is on ...	Invisible factors, eg intelligence, ability, genes, chance.	Dispositional factors, eg perseverance, courage, openness to new learning.
Evidenced in the theories and work of ...	Francis Galton, Lewis Terman, Cyril Burt, Linda Silverman, Miraca Gross, Ellen Winner and even Howard Gardner.	Jean-Jacques Rousseau, Reuven Feuerstein, Carol Dweck, Dona Matthews, Joe Renzulli, Guy Claxton, Robert Sternberg.
Practical applications seen in ...	The 11+, CAT and IQ tests, MENSA, the 'English Framework' of giftedness.	Preparing for the 11+, The TASC Wheel (page 84) and other thinking skills approaches, 'Living Theory' research (pages 112-118).

The 'mystery' framework

The 'mystery' framework relates to the first and most familiar of the two definitions (page 9). It not only *describes* a child's exceptional performances, but it seeks to *explain* them too by calling on invisible (mysterious) concepts such as 'ability', 'intelligence', 'cleverness', and 'brightness'. This invites a sort of circular reasoning:

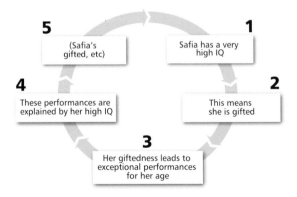

1 Safia has a very high IQ

2 This means she is gifted

3 Her giftedness leads to exceptional performances for her age

4 These performances are explained by her high IQ

5 (Safia's gifted, etc)

This socially dominant framework leads to a test-and-place impulse, based on the belief that we can't do much about the child's native intelligence, but we can provide for her when we know whether or not she's gifted. The 'naturally-gifted' mathematician, musician or chess player will need, therefore, to be identified and then to have his or her needs appropriately met.

The 'mastery' framework

The 'mastery' framework relates to the second, less familiar, definition (page 10). In this, giftedness doesn't exist as a mysterious fixed capacity within Safia's head. Instead, it emerges through the interaction of a wide range of factors that are:

- **Fluid** – they change over time
- **Complex** – they're many, messy and unpredictable
- **Unmeasurable** – you can't give a single 'score' to interacting factors

Giftedness, therefore, emerges from sustained enquiry into an area of personal interest. It reflects the amount and quality of the effort, commitment, creative and strategic thinking invested, and the opportunities offered.

The 'mastery' framework leads to a focus on the sort of provision that results in personal engagement, and to the belief that we can't know if children are 'gifted' until they've had the opportunity to develop and demonstrate these qualities. High-level expertise in mathematics, music or chess (or any other domain) comes from opportunity, commitment, intrinsic motivation, etc.

Implications of the 'mastery framework'

Q: So where does the mastery framework lead your practice?
A: To really exciting and challenging places!

For a start, expect to be working from left to right on these dimensions:

Collecting data (measurement and judgment)	▷	Supporting learning (teaching)
Curriculum acceleration (pace)	▷	Curriculum enrichment/extension (breadth/depth)
A focus on G&T students (cohort identification)	▷	A focus on G&T education (provision)
An emphasis on 'ability' and 'intelligence'	▷	An emphasis on effort and interest
Summative assessment (showing/comparing)	▷	Formative assessment (guiding learning)
Accountability through systems and procedures (summative record-keeping)	▷	Accountability through evidence of pupils' commitment, interest and intrinsic motivation (developmental portfolios)
Short-term performance	▷	Long-term learning (long-term performance)

So standards aren't important then?

This Pocketbook puts the mastery framework at its centre. This requires a valuing of activities that put a primary emphasis on learning, and only a secondary emphasis on performance.

'All well and good, but how can I maintain this focus in the face of a system which puts academic performance above all else?'

At its best, our education system should deliver *both* learning *and* performance. The highest levels of performance in any domain follow an obsession with learning, not a response to someone else's performance demands.

This is true of us as teachers as much as it's true of our pupils, and it's also the direction in which things are moving nationally and abroad. The impressive research evidence underpinning formative assessment strategies and the evidence contributed to and reflected in the Cambridge Review provide just two compelling examples.

The 'Big A' – Accountability

You will be held accountable for your policies and practices in the field of G&T. You should be – not least by your pupils!

But it's also the 'Big A' that drives many outstanding teachers, often against their better judgments, into the dead-ends of traditional mystery framework practices – cohorts, cut-off data, registers, labelling, distinct teaching and learning provision, etc. It needn't do, even when it's the route we're expected to follow. Ultimately, you can be accountable for only one truly compelling question:

Can you provide evidence that your students – including those already performing at a high level – are being appropriately stretched, challenged and extended in their learning?

If you can, you are beyond reproach. But note that word 'evidence'. Evidence can take many forms, performance measurement data being but one. This Pocketbook provides several examples of other ways in which outstanding educators have answered this question, and answered it well.

Small steps – a route to mastery

Gifts and talents, like all learning, emerge through **sustained activity** and **deep reflection**. No-one learns from experience – we learn by *reflecting* on the experience. This takes time, and needs small steps. The same is true if you're looking steadily to move your provision from the mystery model to the mastery model. There's only one way to eat an elephant – one bite at a time!

In the next section of this Pocketbook we will be focusing on the factor that keeps you and your students munching away at the elephant, steadily developing an inclusive approach to gift-creation, developing your gifts and creating the conditions for your students to develop theirs. We'll be looking at internal drive – **intrinsic motivation**.

Mystery or
Mastery?

 Motivation –
Intelligence's
Motor

 Grow!

 Relate!

 Act!

 Challenge!

 Exert!

Motivation – Intelligence's Motor

Your story

Think of an ambition, goal or satisfaction that you've achieved in your life. It could be in any domain – professional/career, academic, sporting, hobby, personal relationship, etc. Now identify *how* you achieved your success. Find a word or short phrase to describe this *'how.'*

Ambition, goal or satisfaction achieved	How I achieved this

Typical responses

I've done this exercise with many thousands of adults and students. I never ask people what their goal or ambition was. I always ask them how they achieved it (whatever 'it' is). Here's what they tell me:

Overwhelmingly popular explanations	Occasional explanations	Rare explanations
Effort; support from others; perseverance; determination; risk-taking; having a go; enjoying the process; patience; coping with obstacles; practice; planning; persistence; making a strategy; encouragement; self-belief; positive self-talk; trying a different approach; thinking about times I've achieved difficult things before; advice; bounce-back-ability; interest in it; imagining myself doing it; working to repay others' faith in me; proving others wrong; constructive feedback; modifying my goals; breaking it down into small steps; having a vision.	Luck, chance, faith, realism.	Natural ability, intelligence, aptitude, a gift or talent.

How do your own responses compare with these?

Your story and others'

> *'The three great essentials to achieve anything worthwhile are: first, hard work; second, stick-to-it-iveness; third, common sense.'* **Thomas Edison**

There may be many explanations for the consistency of the 'your story' findings, not least a British reluctance publicly to attribute personal success to talent, ability or intelligence. Interestingly, however, when this activity is completed anonymously and in writing, identical patterns of responses occur. I have come to a terrible conclusion: **people are telling me the truth!**

What implications do you draw about the relative weight we give to the concept of 'ability' in schools (streaming, setting, banding, G&T cohorts, even mixed-ability classes), and the actual significance we acknowledge in our own lives?

You could use this exercise with your students, or with their parents, as an introduction to a discussion around your mastery-oriented approach to learning, and the growth (not identification) of gifts and talents.

Motivation – extrinsic vs intrinsic

Most explanations people give for reaching a goal relate to motivational factors.

Extrinsic learning motivation relies on an external agent to keep the learner focused. External agents include such things as the three Ps: praise, prizes and performance grades. It is the outcomes of the activity that are rewarding so the activity is focused on the *products* of learning.

Intrinsic learning motivation refers to that hunger to learn that comes from within the learner. It is behaviour driven by such things as intellectual curiosity, creative restlessness and a passion truly to master a skill, puzzle or knowledge domain. The activity itself is satisfying and rewarding. It is focused, therefore, on the *processes* of learning.

Professor Carol Dweck, an eminent developmental psychologist from America, has spent the best part of forty years studying factors that support and inhibit learning and achievement. She describes intrinsic motivation as the 'motor of intelligence' – but remains agnostic as to what exactly intelligence *is*.

Beliefs about ability

Just suppose you'd believed that in order to achieve your goal you had to have natural ability and, by implication, pre-existing eminence in that domain. For instance, if becoming a teacher had been your goal, you already had to have the pre-existent skills to be a *naturally gifted*, wonderfully competent teacher. Would you really have embarked on the journey? And even if you had, would it have meant that much to you? Would you even remember it as having been a goal?

What if, believing you were a naturally gifted teacher, you came up against a class you couldn't teach, or a topic you struggled to explain to them? Would you crumple, doubt your ability and try a new career, or would you kick in with new strategies and improve your practice? How you respond depends on your mindset, ie what you believe about the origins of your teaching skills and talents.

Beliefs about ability – and their effects

Carol Dweck and her colleagues have found that:

- If you believe something to be an inherent, fixed quality (eg fixed ability, giftedness, intelligence), then in the face of difficulties you're more likely to grumble, crumple or cheat!
- If you believe something to be learnable (eg seeing ability, giftedness, intelligence as 'growable') then in the face of difficulties you're more likely to try harder, develop new strategies, etc – and therefore become better at it
- We're fairly evenly split over things like intelligence, ability, etc. About 40% of us incline towards 'fixed' beliefs, and 40% towards 'malleable' beliefs. The rest of us swing from one to the other, dependent on the domain, eg fixed beliefs about our 'maths ability', and malleable beliefs about our DIY skills
- Highly successful people are much more likely to believe that they can always improve – and work hard to do so

Beliefs about giftedness – and their effects

Just like the term 'ability', the term 'giftedness' can be seen as either fixed or malleable ('plastic'). How you see it affects your actions:

It's 'Fixed'	It's 'Plastic'
You believe giftedness is a fixed trait.	You believe giftedness is cultivated through learning.
Your priority is to look smart, not dumb. Get things right, quickly. Don't ask questions. It's about *appearances*, stupid.	Your priority is to become smarter through seeking out challenges and learning – *'who cares what I look like?'*.
You feel smart achieving easy, low effort successes and outperforming others.	You feel smart engaging fully with new tasks, exerting effort, stretching and applying skills.
You avoid effort, difficulty, setbacks, higher-performing peers – *'these all prove I'm stupid.'*	You avoid easy, previously mastered tasks – *'I can't learn from these.'*

The big bad 'fixers' – myths and demons

- As a child, I was terrified of learning my IQ score – the risks were too high
- As an adolescent I was warned that my exam grades would define my future
- As an undergraduate I learned that someone's IQ between infancy and middle age would, on average, differ by five points – attributable to measurement error
- As a postgraduate student in the 1980s I came across a document that set out IQ range requirements for the admission of new students to the university – by faculty!
- As a teacher, my knowledge of my pupils' CAT scores strongly influenced my academic expectations of them
- As a psychologist, I noticed that children's IQ scores remained remarkably stable when tested over time – 'proof' of the fixed nature of intelligence

A reality check

The myths and demons logged on the previous page and that have dogged much of my life are based on spurious, superficial and often self-perpetuating evidence. If we take a reality check, we remember:

- The world is full of school 'dunces' who go on to excel in their chosen domain – and vice versa. **Sustained effort predicts future performance more strongly than 'natural ability'**

- How often as teachers have we been shocked by the sudden spasm of insight and brilliance from a 'bottom-setter'?

- The relative reliability of IQ instruments is a function not of the 'fixed' nature of intelligence but of the fact that children do not routinely practise tasks such as 'block design' or 'recall of digits reversed' between tests. Their scores would improve if they did – but would that matter? I suspect the world would keep on turning at the same speed as it always did

Is giftedness *really* plastic?

You might well be thinking that a belief in the plasticity of giftedness is just some well-meaning, educationally trendy mumbo-jumbo: that the honest-to-God, down 'n' dirty empirical *reality* is that it's fixed.

Well, with a nod to Henry Ford, the interesting thing is that whether you think it is, or whether you think it isn't, you're probably right! If you believe that deep down you've either got it or you haven't, you're less likely to work hard at getting it – and therefore you won't! But if you believe that by immersing yourself in a tough learning situation you'll get smarter, you will.

The same is true of our beliefs about our pupils' abilities. Expect students to rise to tough challenges, and they have a good chance of doing so.

Giftedness – mind your language

*'**Gift**, n: A natural quality, talent, or endowment.'* Concise English Dictionary

Take a moment to reflect on the terminology. The words we use impact hugely on motivational states. Is anything a natural talent? Really?

One of the problems with the word 'gifted' is that it encourages static, fixed, mystery-framework beliefs, ie a gift is something freely given and unearned (children don't earn gifts on their birthdays – they just get them). So does that mean I *am* gifted? Just because? And I don't need actually to do anything about it? I am Mozart. My music will just *emerge*.

Smart giftedness

If you have to use the word 'gifted' (and you might – it's the currently dominant term), try to find smart ways of using it, so that you communicate to students (and parents) that it's a plastic quality. Ensure that they learn:

- That they have *grown* their gifts (or talents) – they haven't just 'happened'
- That they can grow these even further – there's no limit to skills, expertise or knowledge
- That they can grow new gifts – as their interests and motivations change
- That they can 'lose' their gifts – if their interest or commitment wanes
- That to grow gifts, they must be motivated from *within*

'What the research shows consistently is that if you face children with intellectual challenges and then help them talk through the problems towards a solution, you almost literally stretch their minds. They become cleverer, not only in the particular topic, but across the curriculum.' **Prof. Philip Adey** (see page 126).

Intrinsic motivation – a case history

Consider Emma, a gifted mathematician: Emma routinely came top in her class and Year 9 year group, and worked successfully with Year 11 and 12 members of the school's maths club. She represented her school in local Maths Challenge competitions with distinction. Chosen to represent her county in a national Year 9 Maths Olympiad, she expected to do well. By the end of the day, she was unplaced and felt she had let herself, her gender, and her county down.

How would you respond to her?

a. Tell her you thought she'd been unlucky.

b. Tell her she hadn't deserved to excel in the Olympiad.

c. Reassure her that maths isn't a matter of life or death.

d. Tell her she'd got the ability, and she'd win next time.

e. Tell her she'd been robbed of a medal that was rightfully hers.

Emma – your call

Only one of the five response-options provided for Emma has a chance of encouraging the intrinsic learning motivation she needs if she's to cope with this setback and kick on. It's probably the only one she doesn't want to hear, b: that she hadn't deserved to excel in the Olympiad. The other four are all designed to offer her some short-term reassurance, but they're all decidedly questionable in their assurances, or cast doubt on the weight she gives to her passion for maths.

Of course, you wouldn't stop at telling her she didn't deserve to win: you'd help her to figure out *why* she didn't, and what she needed to do to improve. Achievement and eminence are indeed the long-term goals, but she needs to keep a sense of personal agency, and honesty's at the heart of it. If she didn't deserve to win, don't kid her that she did.

(By the way, Emma's story is a true one, and it's also based on research evidence. She was given the above response and, after a lot of hard work, won the following year. I know of many similar stories across the curriculum.)

Praise – core principles

If you want to encourage students' intrinsic learning motivation and the idea that abilities and gifts are learnable and not fixed, it will be important to comment positively on the *processes* of learning **not** on students' 'intelligence,' 'abilities' or 'giftedness.' This isn't because people don't like hyperbolic praise – they often do – but they will come to *need* the praise. This leads to self-doubt, panic, surrender, cheating and the avoidance of challenge and risk-taking when things get tough and the praise dries up. So:

- Praise the behaviour, not the child
- Praise the process, not the product
- Praise the learning, not the performance

Problematic praise

Avoid at all costs superficially positive comments such as these:

✗ *'Intelligence strikes again!'* (Leave that one for the tabloids or blockbusters)

✗ *'Leonie, you're brilliant!'* (She isn't, but her work might be – on this occasion!)

✗ *'You're bright, so you should find this easy'* (So if I find it tough, I'm thick?)

✗ *'I know you can do this – you're a smart cookie'* (Ditto)

✗ *'Come on Adam, you're a very able boy – you should be doing better'*
(Actually he might quite like the label able underachiever – it's cool, and safe!)

✗ *'You're destined for greatness!'* (No-one is!)

Perfect praise

Contrast 'fixed-state praise' of the *'You're smart'* kind with the sorts of comments that focus on the really important factors – the student's learning, commitment, intellectual adventuring and curiosity, seeking of challenges, and toleration of uncertainty and error.

These are the good guys:

✔ *'I like the way you stuck at that problem'*
✔ *'I appreciate your effort'*
✔ *'Fantastic concentration Mark'*
✔ *'Wonderful – tell me what you've learned from these mistakes'*
✔ *'You've chosen something really tough – well done – go for it!'*

These don't scream *'I'm brilliant!'* – as those on the previous page do. And to many students who are hung-up on being seen to be gifted, 'quick' and omniscient, they may seem rather weak and unwelcome. But all these comments help convey an emphasis on the process of learning and its journey-like nature. Stick with them – they'll get through in the end!

Magnificent stories of mediocrity – 'growing gifts'

To emphasise the power of intrinsic motivation to build giftedness, give your students multiple examples of quotations from high profile achievers. Look out for recent examples in the media. Here are my current favourite monuments to the relative insignificance of native gifts and to the power of error, uncertainty, struggle and dogged persistence over time:

- *'What you really need is stick-to-it-iveness. It's a noun. It means dogged persistence. This is what I was taught. I was dyslexic, the least likely to succeed. It means things don't just happen – you have to make them happen.'* (Erin Brockovich, campaigner)
- *'Talent is not enough.'* (Martin Jol, football manager)
- *'If people knew how hard I had to work to achieve my mastery, it wouldn't seem wonderful at all.'* (Michelangelo)
- *'Greatness is not given. It has to be earned.'* (Barack Obama, US President)

Implications for practice

Believing in the plasticity of giftedness and the importance of promoting intrinsic learning motivation has implications for school and classroom practice. So what's 'in' and what's 'out'?

Out	In
Prioritising the **identification** of gifted students – labelling and registers.	Prioritising **provision** – truly personalised learning experiences.
Exclusive provision for identified 'G&T' pupils – exciting opportunities for the few, tedium for the masses.	**Inclusive** provision (initially available to all students).
Fixed cohorts – 5-10% of students based on norm-referenced ability criteria (eg SAT or CAT scores).	**Flexible cohorts** – eg based on student interest and personal application in that area, at that time.
Gifts ('academic' subjects) versus talents ('non-academic' subjects) distinctions.	Recognition that giftedness emerges in all domains, with no arbitrary distinctions, and through substantially the same processes.
A focus on **data**.	A focus on **learning**.

A framework for gift creation

> *'Grace – n., an acquired accomplishment.'* Concise English Dictionary

The next five chapters of this Pocketbook describe the GRACE framework for creating gifts – not just identifying them – within a mastery-oriented, motivational school and classroom.

Grow!   This signature element of the framework captures the fluid, changeable processes at the heart of gift-creation. Gifts are *grown*, not found.

Relate!   Gifts are grown in *relationships* of trust, warmth and mutual respect – not in an emotional vacuum.

Act!   Gifts are grown through engagement in high-order *activity* and reflection on it – this activity might be intellectual and/or physical.

Challenge!   Gifts are grown at and through moments of apparent intellectual *impasse and contradiction*, requiring the making of new connections.

Exert!   Gifts are created slowly, over time and usually after the *exertion* of much hard work, setbacks and false starts.

A framework for gift creation

The elements of the framework support each other – they aren't mutually exclusive.
For the purposes of this Pocketbook I have devoted a chapter to each element.
Each chapter:

- Describes the element
- Suggests ways of nurturing it
- Outlines some implications for school policy
- Links each element to a practical learning tool:

Element	Exemplar Learning Tool
Grow!	LogoVisual Thinking (LVT).
Relate!	Philosophy for Children (P4C).
Act!	Thinking Actively in a Social Context (TASC).
Challenge!	Dilemma-Based Learning (DBL).
Exert!	Living Theory Action Research (LTAR).

Mystery or Mastery?

 Motivation – Intelligence's Motor

 Grow!

 Relate!

 Act!

 Challenge!

 Exert!

Grow!

Description

> 'The thing about performance, even if it's only an illusion, is that it's a celebration of the fact that we do contain within ourselves infinite possibilities.' **Daniel Day-Lewis**

G, standing for Grow!, is the signature element of the GRACE framework. It refers to **the capacity of living things to change into a vast variety of new forms**.

It is the lifeblood of all true educators: the knowledge that we can affect children's lives for the better – and worse. It is the hope that sees the Olympian gymnast beyond the naughty schoolboy (Louis Smith), the inventor beyond the hopeless scholar (Thomas Edison), the tireless campaigner beyond the dyslexic low-achiever (Erin Brockovich), and the sprinter beyond the footless child (Oscar Pistorius).

G – a case history

Some years ago I was told an academic lecturer's history (actually, geography):

- Geography O-level: 'F'
- Retake: 'C'
- Geography A-level: 'E'
- BSc Geography with Physics (Cardiff University): 1st
- PhD (Nottingham University)
- Lecturer in Geography (Durham University)
- Senior Lecturer (Liverpool University)

I've been flooded with many, many similar tales of triumph from the most inauspicious of beginnings. Here's my hunch: even if there'd been such a thing as a school 'G&T register' back in the old days, very few of these folk would have made it onto one. George Bernard Shaw knew it:

> *'Life isn't about finding yourself. Life is about creating yourself.'*

G&T Identification - 0; G&T Creation -1.

Some ways of nurturing G

Here are five ways of helping to nurture the G element with your students in your classroom:

1. Talk at length about *learning* (which the learner does for herself, and which focuses on the process) and less about *work* (which they'll do, reluctantly, for you, and which can fixate on the product).
2. Get your students thinking and talking about change and growth. Ask them to reveal (or make) the higher-order connections between objects and/or pictures like these: lettuce-seeds, tiger-cubs, a rain-drop falling over a mountain, the infant Lewis Hamilton.
3. Use art, drama, music to engage students at all levels. Also trips to museums, shows, galleries, concerts, etc. Expand their boundaries.

Some ways of nurturing G

4. Keep the composition of student working groups fluid and appropriate for specific and time-limited purposes. Think carefully about the group names, especially in the early years. Ditch 'Diamond Group' and 'Coal Group' (solid carbon states) and consider instead names which capture portents of accumulating size and power: Acorns, Cubs, Snowflakes, etc with younger children, or Neurons, Stem Cells, Zygotes, and so on with older students. (There are limits – 'Sperm Group' might be pushing it!)

5. Bring in outside experts to work alongside students. And don't neglect to harness the hidden talents of 'inside experts' among staff and students.

Implications for whole school policy

At a whole school level, the G element has one profound implication, and a number of corollaries:

There should be no fixed cohort of 'G&T' students.

Instead, if a 'cohort' is necessary at all (and remember, a 'cohort' is an ancient battalion of well-drilled soldiers!), consider a number of time-limited student groupings, focused on specific interests, tasks and projects. You could rename these cohorts SIGs – Special Interest Groups or CEGs – Committed Enquiry Groups.

Students should enter and leave the groups with quiet dignity, with neither angelic hosts nor admonishing demons in attendance. Challenge levels should be high – even to the point of 'failure'. Entry and exit should be contingent on such factors as interest, application and toleration of 'failure' (not intelligence, ability, quick success), and, increasingly, the decision of the students themselves.

Talking the walk

To promote the G element in your classroom, it is important to provide your students with frequent examples of real-life journeys to achievement – especially those that seemed unlikely at the outset. There are many such examples in *Millennium People* (see page 126), but look out for similar rags-to-riches tales in magazines, newspapers and weekend supplements, **and tell them**. Emphasise how often the success (in any field) followed years of dedicated involvement in the processes of learning and improvement – not a mysterious moment of waking up 'famous'. Leave the Big Brother celebrity moments where they belong.

Most powerfully of all, tell your own story. Talk your own walk. You may not be a Robbie Williams or a Christine Ohuruogu (yet), but you'll have your own tale to tell and your students will probably relate more immediately to that than to many more famous journeys. Who are you? What are your own gifts, talents and achievements? How did you make them? Are you who you thought you were going to be? What are your current goals and ambitions? What are you doing about achieving them? Ask your students to set *you* targets!

A predictive route-map

Many successful people in life talk about having made themselves a route-map for their lives when they were young. Get your students to do the same:

My age now	My current skills, interests and achievements

Who/what I want to be by 30

My next step to get there? (A realistic short-term target)

How will I make my next step? (List 3 specific things I can – and will – do, and when I'll do them by)

1		by
2		by
3		by

Generating G through LogoVisual Thinking (LVT)

One of the ways you can translate the G element in gift-creation into classroom practice is through the approach known as LogoVisual Thinking, or LVT. This is the name given to a methodology and associated tools that permit thinking to be made visible. The three components of LVT are:

- Logo – articulating discrete units of meaning in words and icons
- Visual – revealing and manipulating patterns and connections
- Thinking – attaining new levels of understanding or perception

Pupils capture their ideas individually on pieces of card, post-its, or magnetic notes (see page 56). Working in groups they then sort and organise their ideas conceptually and visually, drawing on such high-order processes as analysis, connection-making, evaluation, etc. The end-product is conceptually 'bigger' than the starting materials.

LVT can lead to the co-creation of new meanings and ways of seeing things. Insights and possibilities grow and deepen. It supports very elegantly the G element of the GRACE framework.

What are the core aims of LVT?

LVT aims to confer a range of benefits to students:

- To engage learners of all abilities, and indeed to mess with the traditionally-defined construct of 'ability'
- To help them make sense of complex information
- To enhance their thinking capacity
- To aid their articulation and communication of ideas
- To enable groups to learn through interaction

For you and your school, LVT aims to develop the learning context (lesson design, continuity, curriculum transfer) and the thinking capacity of the school as a whole. LVT resonates with many aspects of current educational reform, supporting more collaborative, process-rich and inclusive types of activity. Because many characteristics of the method will be familiar to you and your colleagues, you'll be quick to pick up on its potential.

What does LVT involve?

The LVT process consists of the following stages:

Stage	Description	Core question
1. Focus	Set a guiding question, selected from a topic area.	What are we going to think about?
2. Gather	Collect ideas from memory, association, imagination or prompts.	What do we know about it?
3. Organise	Sort into groups, clusters or themes.	What sense can we make of it?
4. Understand	Make meaning – see the ideas as a unity.	What does it all add up to?
5. Apply	Work towards a product, eg an essay or story, a play, poster, etc.	What can we make of it?

The tools of LVT

LVT can make use of a variety of equipment, from home-made pieces of card, cheap-as-chips sticky notes, pricier 'Post-it®' hexagons (which tessellate in useful ways) through to magnetic hexagons (MagNotes) with whiteboards and Visual Concept software (which can be emailed, or exported as text or graphic files into word-processing software).

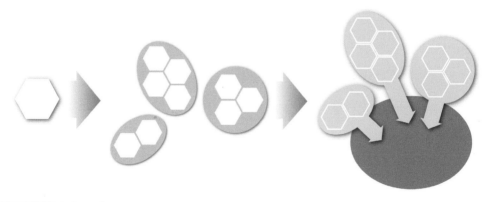

What does LVT look like in the classroom?

LVT can be used right across the age range and in all curriculum areas.

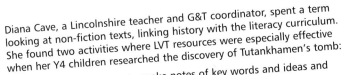

Diana Cave, a Lincolnshire teacher and G&T coordinator, spent a term looking at non-fiction texts, linking history with the literacy curriculum. She found two activities where LVT resources were especially effective when her Y4 children researched the discovery of Tutankhamen's tomb:

1. They used MagNotes to make notes of key words and ideas and then ordered them chronologically.

2. They then collected ideas from various sources (Gathering), collaboratively mapped their information (Organise and Understand), and then used this LVT map to write a piece of connected prose (Application).

The children's individual and collective 'meaning' grew with each stage and the final products were far richer, deeper and more connected than they might otherwise have been.

Used with permission

How can I find out more about LVT?

Seminal resource

Making Meaning – Learning through logovisual thinking by Brin Best, Anthony Blake and John Varney. Published by Chris Kington Publishing, 2005

The key reference for LVT is the dedicated website www.logovisual.com run by the Centre for Management Creativity who pioneered the development of LVT tools and processes. The website provides articles and references to many examples of LVT applications in educational settings, as well as access to training and resources.

LVT Thinking Skills Guidebook by Brin Best. Published by Centre for Management Creativity, 2002.

LVT Knowledgebase, Numerous articles and examples of classroom practice can be found online at **www.logovisual.com/knowledgebase**

Mystery or Mastery?

 Motivation – Intelligence's Motor

 Grow!

 Relate!

 Act!

 Challenge!

 Exert!

Relate!

Description

'All true living is meeting.' **Martin Buber**

The R element of the framework is the secret weapon in the gift-creating teacher's armoury. It is **the recognition that individuals will strive to be who they could ideally be in relationships of trust, regard and mutual respect.** It is the R element that sees gifts grow and bloom with one teacher, yet wither or fail to germinate with another.

R is not to be found in the content-knowledge of the teacher or in the efficiency with which they disseminate their knowledge, but in their emotional connections, the rapport they establish with their students.

In the words of Carl Jung: *'The curriculum is so much raw material, but warmth is the vital element for the growing plant and the soul of the child'.*

R – case histories

The following extracts come from an on-line forum concerned with 'high-ability' children:

'This academic year our very bright 6-year-old son is absolutely loving school. Why, after two years of absolute trauma, boredom and deliberate misbehaviour, has our son become a motivated, excited, learning-driven child? I put it down to one thing: the teacher. She likes him ....'
Mother on high-ability list, on-line forum, December 2004

'The enrichment tasks teachers write can be very challenging and inspiring, but if they fail to motivate, give just and fair feedback, and approach the kids as seriously as they do their friends and colleagues, then the whole project very often fails.'
Heleen Wientjes, Utrecht University, high-ability list, December 2004

Some ways of nurturing R

Here are three ways of developing the R element of the framework:

1. At some point in the school year, write a letter to each child in your class. Personalise it so that it can only apply to that particular child. Refer to their interests, hobbies, personality and strengths. Express your (unconditional) high regard for that child, and your hopes that through commitment and self-motivation they'll work to achieve their aims in that school year and beyond.

2. Ask each child in your class to teach you something by the end of the school year. Within professional limits, it doesn't matter what the something is: to improve your texting speed, to dance like you're not a teacher (!) ... Log the event-date and skill/knowledge acquired. Thank your teacher.

3. Begin each morning/lesson with a greeting, and a question: *'How are things going for you today?'* Listen to their answers. (If you already do this, every day, apologies if that sounds patronising; if you don't, it's just advice – from my school-age daughters, who notice things.)

Nurturing R by valuing questions

'A good question is one half of wisdom.' **Sir Francis Bacon**

Classrooms that encourage student questioning tend also to encourage the growth of a risk-free learning ethos, where respectful relationships between students and teacher are strongly in evidence.

Create a Wonder-Wall or Thought-Board – a small area of display surface on which students' own questions are stuck and affirmed. Teachers do **not** need to 'answer' the questions when these are asked – or indeed later. They need to value them: thank the student for the question and ask for it to be written down on a scrap of paper and placed on the thought-wall.

Later that lesson/day/week, refer to the thought-wall and ask affirming questions such as, *'What sparked this question?'*, *'What could be done to answer it?'*, *'What implications does it have?'*, *'How does it connect to our area/s of study?'* In this way, students learn that the smart thing is to ask good questions, not just to provide answers to them.

Wonder-Wall

Implications for whole school policy

Here are three significant implications for developing the R element within your school:

1. The G&T (or SIG, or CEG – see page 50) policy should dovetail with other relevant policies and subject areas, eg SEAL, PSHE, anti-bullying policy, etc). Are the links explicit?

2. Consider the emotional climate of the school, from the students' points of view: ask them on a no-names basis to identify the qualities they most like and respect in a teacher. Collate this information, and show it to your colleagues. Discuss its implications in a staff meeting. Act on the outcomes and monitor the effects.

3. Note where this quotation comes from: *'The school/college places equal emphasis on high achievement and emotional well-being …'*
   (National Quality Standards in G&T, section D 9 (ii) – Exemplary Level.)

Generating R through Philosophy for Children (P4C)

'...the only true gift is a portion of yourself.' **Ralph Waldo Emerson**

Philosophy for Children or P4C is a process whereby teacher and students regularly come together to explore issues philosophically. The 'P' of P4C is not the philosophy of academia, but a narrative philosophy that emphasises quality dialogue, careful deliberation, good judgment, and the growth of a 'community of enquiry'. In P4C the teacher escapes the role of *knowing transmitter* or instructor, and instead takes a 'fallibilistic' co-enquiring role. Their job (and it is rightly a tough job) is to facilitate good and caring thinking within the community.

Experienced facilitators invariably speak of how P4C helps them to come to know their students so much better, and to relate to them with far greater insight. And vice versa. One teacher told me that after her first P4C enquiry a student said:

> 'I really liked this. Everyone listened to me – even the teacher'.

P4C is a powerful way to generate the R element of the GRACE framework.

What are the core aims of P4C?

Several core aims underpin the P4C approach, all of which have practical implications. Here are a few:

Aim	Implication
To improve students' reasoning ability.	Students are required to reason things through, using evidence and example.
To develop students' creativity.	Unorthodox ideas are welcomed and encouraged, but also examined and improved.
To support students' personal and interpersonal growth.	Students and facilitator treat each other with respect, within a climate that is open and empathic.
To develop students' ethical understanding.	A method of ethical inquiry is emphasised, not a set of ethical rules or 'schemes of work'.
To help students to find meaning in their own experience.	Students connect their experiences to others' and to the 'bigger picture'.

What does P4C involve?

P4C has a 'deep structure' that characterises each enquiry, although each stage can be modified at the surface to suit the group's needs. The core elements are:

1. A short stimulus (picture-book, artefact, story, piece of music…) is presented.
2. Thinking time is provided.
3. In pairs/small groups students share their thoughts and generate a question.
4. Each pair's/group's question is written up and publicly aired.
5. Connections between questions are identified and explored.
6. The students vote democratically, and one question is selected as the focus for the whole-class enquiry.
7. Seated in a circle, the chosen question is explored by the class, with the facilitator probing for connections and distinctions between concepts, seeking reasons, evidence, examples and counter-examples of students' opinions, views and beliefs, etc.
8. A 'last words' round brings the enquiry to a (provisional) closure.
9. Ideally, there is a plenary reflection on the process – how well did we do, and how can we do even better next time?

Good practice in P4C – a few pointers

For the facilitator of P4C, here are just a few good practice suggestions:

- Learn to distinguish between a discussion (an airing of multiple views, beliefs, ideas etc) and a philosophical enquiry (a forward momentum, leading to new insights, connections, distinctions, understandings of terms and concepts, etc). Aim for the latter

- Master the tools of good facilitation – questions that clarify terms *('What do you mean by ...?')*, probe for reasons and evidence *('Why do you think that ...?')*, reveal new ideas *('Does anyone have a different point of view?')*, test for implications and consequences *('So what follows from this?')*, and promote meta-cognition *('What have we been thinking about today?')*

- Tolerate silence – in the enquiry and from individual students. Silence can be both a spur and a watering-hole to thought, and the silent students are often the ones most engaged in the process

The P4C Pocketbook co-written with Roger Sutcliffe offers a concise and practical introduction to P4C.

What might P4C look like in the infant classroom?

Primary school case study

A class of 5 – 7 year olds enjoyed the story 'The Day Jake Vacuumed' by Simon James. Their questions included, 'How did he suck the place so white when he was still in a house?' and 'Why did he want to get into BIG trouble, instead of just trouble?' The resultant discussion covered possible distinctions between trouble and BIG trouble, the nature of 'trouble' and the children's personal tussles between 'being good' and the lure of the forbidden.

Young children are quite capable of exploring conceptually rich domains of knowledge, and with encouragement can begin to use reason and evidence in their arguments, and appropriate terminology too, terms and phrases such as: 'connection', 'distinction', 'I agree/disagree with … because …', 'It doesn't follow that …' etc.

And in the secondary classroom?

CASE STUDY

Secondary school case study

Gorden Pope is the G&T Adviser for the London Borough of Lewisham. His first enquiry on completion of his P4C Level 1 training was with a Year 9 group. He used an extract from the Mad Hatter's Tea Party to generate a discussion on the nature of time. There were some puzzled looks to begin with, but once the question-generating small groups got going, he could overhear their shifts into the realm of abstract concepts. Their questions, in order of popularity:

- 'Why does time feel like it passes at different speeds?'
- 'Why did they ask Alice a riddle if they didn't know the answer themselves?'
- 'Why was there such a big table?'
- 'Why does the Hatter have a clock that tells the year but doesn't say what o'clock it is?'
- 'Why do they refer to time as a person?'

- 'How can you control time?'
- 'What is the theme of Alice in Wonderland?'
- 'Where do such ideas for a story come from?'

P4C 'time' enquiry

Ground covered in Gorden's 'time' enquiry included:

- The meridian line
- Who invented seconds and minutes and the reasons for 60 (not 100) minutes in an hour (invitation to research into Babylonian maths?)
- The reality of time
- The perception of the passing of time. The idea that enjoyment makes 'time fly' was turned on its head with the proposition that something unpleasant but complex could also accelerate the perception of time (flow states?)

Students' last words

Students' comments from the 'last words' round of Gorden's enquiry included:

'It was interesting but confusing. I didn't think we'd get so much out of a simple question.'

'It doesn't matter what the time is; it's how you use it.'

'The sun is time.'

'You can't go back and change time – use what you've got – in 30 years' time … .'

'Time is not real. It's not even an illusion; it's just made up. It's a worldwide agreement to organise everyone.'

'I'm still going to think what I think, but it's made me more aware of what other people think.'

How can I find out more about P4C?

Seminal resource

Thinking Together – Philosophical Inquiry for the Classroom by Philip Cam.
Published by Hale & Iremonger Pty Ltd, 1995

**But Why? Teachers Manual: Developing
Philosophical Thinking in the Classroom**
by S. Stanley. Network Educational Press Ltd,
2004 (excellent for Foundation Stage to KS2)

Do You Think What You Think You Think?
By J. Baggini and J. Stangroom. Granta
Publications, 2006

P4C Pocketbook by B. Hymer and R.
Sutcliffe. Teachers' Pocketbooks, 2012

**The Pig That Wants to be Eaten – and 99
other thought experiments** by
J. Baggini. Granta Publications, 2005

Philosophy in the Classroom by Lipman
et al. Temple University Press, 1980

The Philosophy Files by S. Law. Orion
Children's Books, 2004

**Socratic Circles – Fostering Critical and
Creative Thinking in Middle and High School**
by M. Copeland. Stenhouse, 2005

**Teaching Thinking: Philosophical Enquiry in
the Classroom** by R. Fisher. Continuum, 2003

Thinking in Education by M. Lipman.
Cambridge Univ. Press, 2003

The Society for the Advancement of Philosophical Enquiry & Reflection in Education (SAPERE) runs
high-quality introductory and follow-on courses in P4C: **www.sapere.org.uk**

Excellent commercial site with useful material for P4C enquires at all key stages: **www.p4c.com**

Mystery or Mastery?

 Motivation – Intelligence's Motor

 Grow!

 Relate!

 Act!

 Challenge!

 Exert!

A c t !

Description

> 'Creativity is merely a plus name for regular activity ... any activity becomes creative when the doer cares about doing it right, or better.' **John Updike**

The A element of the framework refers **not only to the physical, motor, kinaesthetic act, but also to the invisible, internal, mental activity that characterises reflective thought and learning.**

The A element flourishes, therefore, when meaning is being made, ie when purposeful activity makes way for reflection and the insights which arise from this reflection.

The A element is the performance of the science experiment and the simultaneous or consequent reflection on it – it is not being told a scientific 'truth' and then writing this down in an exercise book. Or in the words of a ten-year-old:

'Learning is asking questions and finding things out, not answering questions – that's knowing.'

A – a case history

Joe, aged ten, disengaged and a relatively low achiever in junior school, once chanced upon a TV programme about a charity in rural India that made inexpensive but effective artificial prostheses. It sparked an interest that he alluded to in a learning journal, which his class teacher had introduced.

The teacher converted this spark into a raging bonfire: with parental support, she introduced Joe to an elderly Quaker, also named Joe, who'd been a volunteer with the Red Cross in Vietnam and who'd developed in that grim context a remarkable expertise in creating prostheses for civilians from basic materials – including bomb-casings.

The friendship between the two Joes grew over the years, divided by age but united by a shared interest, activity-engagement, and value-set. Now in his late 20s, Joe Junior is a qualified and highly accomplished bio-medical engineer, living a fulfilled life. His former class teacher may not know this.

Some ways of nurturing A

Here are three ways of developing the A element of the framework:

1. **Envisioning**. Teach your students how to 'see' themselves doing and completing an activity, before they begin. How do they want the activity to begin, and what should/could it look like while they're doing it? How should it end? What could go wrong? What would a successful completion of the activity look like? Envisioning can be supported by stilling and guided relaxation and visualisation procedures (see Jennifer Day's and Mary Stone's books on page 125).

2. **Meta-learning**. Keep your students focused on the 'learning' within an activity. Paul Bytheway's Meta-Menus (pp 95-98) can help here, but any questions which focus the students on the learning can do too: *'What are the easy/hard bits – and why?'*; *'What's the 'big idea' in this activity?'*; *'How can you relate this activity to other things you've done and learned from?'*, etc.

3. **Authentic audiences**. Create real reasons for work – eg cooking meals for invited parents or canteen staff, preparing and presenting a report to governors, composing a musical score for a special event, etc.

The ASDA Challenge

The **ASDA** challenge (**A**re **S**tudents **D**ormant or **A**ctive?) also helps to nurture A. From time to time in the lesson, randomly choose a student to respond to an ASDA Challenge: ask them to load their thoughts or questions, however brief or limited, on a 'Pay Here' counter (conveying accountability for their own learning).

In the early days, or for less confident students, you could use a 'Learning Receipt' which students fill in, sign and return to you. In due course, or for more confident or younger students, just ask them to tell you (and the class) what they're thinking. It doesn't have to be smart, erudite, or 'correct' – it's the process itself that engages, and some of the best learning (for you and them) comes from the more awkward thoughts, questions and responses.

It's a no-failure, no-blame strategy: even the blank receipts provide opportunities to *talk about learning*: *'What's happening here?'*; *'How could I engage you better?'*; *'How could you engage with me better?'* You're capturing and exploring the process of a learning activity – the fleeting thoughts – because in ASDA when they're gone, they're gone.

The activity of personalised enquiry

Encouraging students to enquire deeply into areas of personal interest and value is a powerful way of fostering the A element. The process of enquiry is consistent with a mastery framework of giftedness because both contain these inherent qualities:

- **Personalised input** – we enquire into things we are interested in, and we grow the gifts we value
- **Opportunities to collaborate** with others – 'None of us is as smart as all of us'
- **The telling of a story** – as a species, we learn well through the power of narrative, and all enquiries can take the form of a story-based narrative
- **The valuing of error** – missed stitches, loose threads and unexpected patterns all become woven into the fabric of the story
- **A valuing of process over product** – we delight in the giving, not just the gift
- **A deep sense of achievement** – we value most the things we worked hardest for, not the things we grasped most easily

Implications for whole school policy

'There are two ways of being creative. One can sing and dance. Or one can create an environment in which singers and dancers flourish.' **Warren Bennis**

Here are three significant implications for developing the A element within your school as a whole:

1. There needs to be a good mix of activities in lessons, employing a range of different learning modalities, senses and challenges, for all pupils (**not** 'visual' activities for the 'visual learners', 'auditory' activities for the 'auditory learners', 'gifted' activities for the 'gifted learners', etc).

2. A stand-alone activity is incomplete. It is completed by the opportunity to reflect deeply on the activity and to plan for improved performances when experiencing similar activities in the future. Is this built into teacher planning?

3. Innovative and experimental learning and teaching activities should be embraced, and critically evaluated.

Generating A through TASC

> 'It is good to rub and polish our brains against those of others.' **Montaigne**

TASC – **T**hinking **A**ctively in a **S**ocial **C**ontext – is a universal framework that allows the content of all curriculum areas to be used as the raw material for developing problem-solving and thinking skills. It draws on a wide theoretical base and is attractively accessible to time-starved classroom teachers.

Students enjoy the active, hands-on opportunities for exploration and enquiry that the approach offers. They are also invited to engage in the discipline of deep reflection which leads to the creative transfer of learning.

TASC represents the A element of the GRACE framework at its most vibrant.

What are the core aims of TASC?

The TASC approach is based on four core dimensions of learning, each harnessed in support of a broad aim:

- **Thinking** – TASC aims to help students to see evidence of their mounting power as thinkers and problem-solvers
- **Actively** – It promotes active participation in decision-making with the aim of supporting understanding of real-life learning processes and the growth of intrinsic motivation
- **Social** – Since no-one is an island, TASC aims to develop skills of interdependence, collaboration and cooperation
- **Context** – TASC aims to support the extension of learning from students' immediate environments to wider social, cultural and global contexts, requiring connection-making at all stages

What does TASC look like?

The TASC process is based around an action research 'problem-solving wheel'

© Belle Wallace (2000), used with permission

The TASC wheel – stages and purposes

The TASC-wheel involves the following stages and purposes:

Stage	Purpose
Gather/ Organise	To collect existing facts and understandings from students and establish 'wholeness' or fragmentation of this knowledge base.
Identify	To clarify the nature of the task and establish key questions.
Generate	To encourage creative 'green hat' thinking and a risk-taking atmosphere where multiple ideas are considered.
Decide	To promote higher-order thinking involving critical, analytic and evaluative skills in order to prioritise, plan and prepare to implement.
Implement	To put their plans into action, using any relevant methods, techniques, modalities and domains.
Evaluate	To establish appropriate criteria for judging the value and success of their work.
Communicate	Through an appropriate mode of presentation to a real audience, to refine and clarify their learning.
Learn from experience	To consolidate and transfer the learning through reflection on the relevant skills acquired and the effectiveness of the problem-solving processes used.

What does TASC look like in the classroom?

Walter Humphries used TASC to explore story with students aged 10–11 over a period of a fortnight. Texts used included *The Last Wolf* by Michael Morpurgo, Norse myth, fairy tale and *Warrior Scarlet* by Rosemary Sutcliff.

Gather/Organise. The children mind-mapped what they knew about wolves, making connections between ideas. Words such as 'sly', 'cunning', 'menace', 'big eyes', 'greedy' and 'howling at midnight' revealed the influence of folktale.

Identify. Pupils generated questions, eg: 'What do wolves mainly eat?'; 'How long do they survive?'; 'Are there wolves in Wales?'; 'How like dogs are they?'

Generate and Decide. Practical issues – resources, pupil numbers and timescales – were discussed in pairs and a decision was made to have individuals or groups researching different aspects of the topic and feeding back to the others. This 'jigsaw' approach saw 'expert groups' researching body facts, diet, family life, environment, the wolf in fable, etc.

What does TASC look like in the classroom?

Implement. Drama techniques, including hot-seating and thought-tracking, were used to focus on the children's interest in the concept of 'wolfness'. How can you understand a wild animal? What is the essence of a wolf? Are wolves like people at all? Pupils improvised scenes where 'wolf-like' children were put into a range of domestic and school situations, allowing the 'inner wolf' to emerge in different ways. The drama led easily into links with the core texts and into the children's own writing, developing themes they'd explored together.

Evaluate. Evaluating their work, children commented: *'I learned how to work in a team and cooperate'*; *'We learned how to work with one another as one and how to feel emotions'*; *'I learned how to think like a wolf and act like one too'*.

Communicate and Learn from Experience. Groups presented their work and class discussed and explored messages and implications for future practice.

Walter found the TASC Wheel framework gave students the necessary structure and support to explore their thoughts and feelings creatively and imaginatively.

(For a fuller description of the project, see *Gifted Education International*, vol 24, pp 255-257, 2008)

How can I find out more about TASC?

Seminal resources

Teaching Thinking Skills Across the Middle Years – A practical approach for children aged 9-14 by Belle Wallace and Richard Bentley. Published by David Fulton Publishers Ltd, 2002

Teaching Thinking Skills Across the Primary Curriculum by Belle Wallace. Published by David Fulton Publishers Ltd, 2001

Thinking Skills and Problem-Solving: An Inclusive Approach – A practical guide for teachers in primary schools by Belle Wallace et al. Published by David Fulton Publishers Ltd, 2004

For training in the TASC method, contact the originator, Belle Wallace at
www.tascwheel.com

Mystery or
Mastery?

 Motivation –
Intelligence's
Motor

 Grow!

 Relate!

 Act!

 Challenge! ◀

 Exert!

Challenge!

Description

> 'Without contraries [there] is no progression.' **William Blake**

Challenge – the C element – can be described as **a tendency for gifts and talents to be created through moments of intellectual contradiction, requiring the making of new connections**. It invites the teacher to embrace opportunities for cognitive conflict, for challenge, doubt and uncertainty, recognising that learning happens most readily when we are intellectually and emotionally open to contradiction – to incompatible facts, events and interpretations.

The C element is the grit in the oyster giving rise to the pearl. It is the reframing of failure as an 'unexpected outcome' and the spur to the creation of new ideas, new explanations and new understandings. It is, therefore, what underpins the relentless advancement of knowledge. It is also central to a mastery-oriented approach to gift-creation.

C – a case history conundrum

You might know that final, spoken, 'Dear Sir' track on an early Robbie Williams album, his recollection of an encounter with a particular teacher at secondary school. This teacher poured scorn, as he recalls, on his ambitions to be a pop star. His retort, *'F- you sir, I will.'* was a contradiction spoken and then lived.

I once met one of Robbie's former classmates. It seems Robbie wasn't the only one to have cold water poured on his hopes by this teacher. It got me thinking. For every student with a growth mindset who turns scorn into ambition and goes on to live their ambitions, how many students with fixed mindsets accept the scorn as true, and go on to live their lives in the shadows of their hopes and aspirations? And what was eating that teacher? A fixed mindset of his own?

Perhaps there's a message here: heap derision on your students' ambitions and await their contradiction as their lives unfold – a brilliant double-bluff, if the pupil holds a growth mindset! A less risky alternative? Exhort your students to strain every sinew in seeking to achieve their goals, but to have back-up plans. A back-up plan can reveal itself as the unknown ambition. (Watch the film *Mr Holland's Opus.*)

Some ways of nurturing C

Here are three ways of helping to nurture the **C** element with your students:

1. Delay closure by soliciting alternative answers and playing devil's advocate. Replace *'That's right'* with *'Why do you say that?'*, and replace *'Well done'* with *'Has anyone got a different point of view?'*.

2. Model it. Show that you learn best by being challenged. Encourage your students to challenge you. Award a star each time you are well challenged. Better still, ask the class to nominate the person they think challenged you best that week, and present that student with a 'Master Contradictor of the Week' certificate which specifies exactly why they merited the award.

3. Create a Challenge Wall. Ask your students to post their own challenges on a display surface. You *don't* have to answer them – that's their job – and the process of setting the challenge is valuable in itself! Newspapers often host such columns: readers write in with queries, and other readers respond. The *Little Book of Thunks* and *100 Intriguing Questions for Kids (Adults too!)* are great starter-resources. (See page 125.)

Nurturing C: the '5-minute challenge'

Ask your students to be prepared to speak to the class for up to five minutes at some time during the term. They can choose to speak on any topic (within or preferably outside the curriculum) as long as they meet the following essential criteria:

- They are genuinely interested (preferably passionate) about the topic, and this shows in the presentation
- They have done some independent research on the topic – via the internet, library, site or museum visit, etc, and this shows
- They are open to questions, challenges and constructive observations from the rest of the class, and can respond appropriately

If possible, ask the students themselves to evaluate their own performances and to highlight their learning points.

Implications for whole school policy

There are a number of ways the C element could impact on whole school G&T policy. Here are three:

1. Challenge should be promoted throughout the curriculum: invest in resources, approaches and thinking tools that regularly take (all) students out of their comfort zones. See page 125 for ideas.

2. Find ways of getting students thinking about their thinking and learning about their learning – Paul Bytheway's Meta-menus on the next few pages are outstanding classroom resources for supporting the development of meta-cognitive (thinking about thinking) and meta-learning (learning about learning) processes.

3. Connect 'G&T' to Assessment for Learning. AfL supports both challenge and metacognition and keeps all students taking responsibility for their own learning journeys.

Meta-menus – a personal contradiction

On a course I was once leading, I was politely challenged by a young teacher. It was clear he didn't much like the 'meta-questions' I was recommending he use with his students. He didn't think they'd excite his students. I asked him to do better. He did, and he sent me the resulting Meta-menus. They're about 100% better than my original version, and they come (overleaf) with Paul Bytheway's permission to plagiarise, modify and use. Some teachers laminate the meta-courses and make a fan of three for each pupil.

At certain points in the lesson (around the beginning, middle and end), students are invited to do a think-pair-share, to:

- Reflect on the menu and choose a starter (or main course, or dessert)
- Tell their partner why they've chosen it
- Reflect on/discuss their partner's choice

The teacher concludes each brief meta-reflection by asking a student to share their course with the whole class. Genius – and simple (the best inventions are both).

Meta-starters

Meta-
STARTERS

What do you want to learn today?

What skills do you have that could be useful this lesson?

What might hinder your thinking?

When have you had to think like this before?

What have you learnt that is similar?

What do you already know that might be useful?

What *must* you do in this lesson? What *should* you do?
What *could* you do?

Meta-main courses

Meta-
MAIN COURSES

What are you currently thinking about?
Has any of the lesson so far been about you?
What connections have you made?
How do you feel about the lesson?
How have you got involved in the lesson?
What should you do to further your thinking?
What breakthroughs have you made?
What do you want to know more about?

Meta-desserts

Meta-
DESSERTS

How are you going to remember this learning?

What is the key aspect you will remember from this lesson?

What has this lesson reminded you of?

Which senses were most important?

What did you learn that you didn't know before?

What have you learnt that could be useful elsewhere?

What have you learned elsewhere that is like this?

How will you apply what you have learnt?

Generating C through Dilemma Based Learning (DBL)

'The vast majority of problems, decisions and situations which confront us daily are those which do not have just one answer. Several solutions are usually possible. Logic suggests that if one can mentally generate many possible solutions, the more likely it is that an optimum solution will be reached. This is a creative process – the formation of new and useful relationships.' **Richard E. Manelis**

Created by Deb Michel, Phil Wood and myself, Dilemma Based Learning is a relatively new thinking tool but one which draws on aspects of many other approaches – eg Socratic questioning, de Bono's Hats, Problem-Based Learning, Mysteries, etc. It involves presenting groups of students with a realistic dilemma (either from a resource bank or self-created) and inviting them to work collaboratively towards a solution through the application of a series of 'Wise Webs'. The Webs and other devices (eg the 'spanner') are designed to generate cognitive conflict, doubt and uncertainty in situations of richly layered complexity.

DBL is a powerful generator of the C element in the GRACE framework.

What does DBL look like?

A DBL lesson can take many forms, but in its simplest application the following stages are involved:

1. Whole class: calming/stilling activity (see Mary Stone's and Jennifer Day's books on page 125).
2. Whole class: presentation of the dilemma.
3. Small group (4-7 students per group): enquiry into the dilemma, using the Think Web, Me Web, Others Web, Community Web, Balance Web.
4. Individual and small group: completion of process review sheet and reflective discussion.
5. Whole class: content and process plenary.

At Stage 3 group members might take on particular roles – eg Webmaster (who manages the Webs), Timekeeper, Facilitator (mediator of the process), Observer (who'll oversee stage 4 reflections), Scout (gleaner of other groups' discussions who reports back pertinent issues to their own group).

What are the core aims of DBL?

There are a number of core aims underpinning the DBL approach. These aims have practical implications. Here are a few:

Aim	Implication
To foster students' toleration of open-ended situations, contrary viewpoints, ambiguity and uncertainty.	Dilemmas are deliberately open-ended and loosely structured, to promote higher-level thinking and social exchange.
To reinforce in students the realisation that (only) they are responsible for their own learning.	The teacher resists students' requests for the 'right' answer, and gives process feedback not product praise.
To develop students' social learning skills.	Difficulties arising from poor social skills are addressed by the group as part of the learning process.
To promote deep understanding of key concepts.	It takes time to tease out the central issues. A 'rush to the reveal' is resisted.

Good practice in DBL – characteristics of a good dilemma

Working with teachers on the writing of their own (often subject-specific) dilemmas, a number of key ingredients have emerged:

- **Someone in the scenario must make a tough choice** – there's no one 'right way' of responding
- **A starter 'hook'** – to maximise interest and engagement, create scenarios that students can to relate to, ideally within their immediate experience
- **Multiple options** – the best dilemmas are rich in possibilities for creative responses
- **'Vivid vagueness'** – when the dilemma lacks great detail a wider range of responses is possible and higher order and counter-factual (*'What if …'*) thinking are called upon
- **'The spanner'** – there is potential to re-generate cognitive conflict by throwing a spanner in the works at a later point in the process, ie a new, critical piece of information that requires a reconsideration of options being mooted
- **Resources are considered** – a good dilemma might have resource implications, eg ethnographic data, lab results, character details, etc – which can be provided *on request by the group* (when they realise these might be helpful)

An example

Lizzy was in Year 6. She had one older sister, Tracy. Not only was Tracy clever, but she was really beautiful – everyone said so. It was getting close to Year 6 SATs. Lizzy thought how great it would be if she could do as well as Tracy – or even better than her. But Lizzy was predicted to scrape level 4s in everything – nothing to worry about, but nothing special either.

Lizzy had arranged to go round to her friend Steph's house to study for the science SAT. She met Steph outside the school gate. Steph was very excited. She took Lizzy to one side and gave her a brown envelope. Inside there was an official-looking science paper. *'It was just sitting there on Miss Khan's desk,'* Steph said. *'Put it in your bag so nobody can see it. Come on.'* Lizzy looked back towards the school. She could see Miss Khan through the glass door. She was rummaging through the papers on her desk looking worried and upset.

(Possible 'spanner': On closer inspection, it turns out that Steph had found a paper from a previous year, not the paper they'd be sitting.)

Using Wise Webs to address Lizzy's dilemma

1. **Think Web**. What makes this a dilemma? Have I experienced anything similar in my life? How many possible solutions can we find? Are any of these solutions linked in some way? Are there any 'whacky' solutions? Trying to select the three most practical solutions from the ones generated we'll need to ask further questions, eg Can any of these solutions be dismissed immediately? Are we sure? What exactly is involved in each solution? What are the implications? What would success or failure look like? What are the costs – to Lizzy's friendship with Steph, her relationship with her teacher? etc.

2. **Me Web**. How does everyone in the group feel about the three 'best' solutions we've come up with? Any objections? On what grounds? How would Lizzy feel about each of the chosen solutions? What implications does it have for her?

3. **Others Web**. Which other characters might be affected? Steph and Miss Khan clearly, but could there be others directly or indirectly affected? Parents? Classmates? Even Tracy? How could each chosen option impact on these other characters? How would they feel, or react?

Using Wise Webs to address Lizzy's dilemma

4. **Community Web**. A community could be a large or small unit: a class, a school, a family, a town, etc. What are the relevant communities in this dilemma? How could each community be affected by the chosen options? What are the long-term implications? What if everyone behaved in this way?

5. **Balance Web**. This final Web allows for a reflective and balanced choice. An intuitive response might well be appropriate, given the complexity of data that's emerged. Take a minute's quiet thinking time, and think about what people have said about each option. Intuition is often at its sharpest after periods of contemplation. What does each group member feel is the best option to go for, and why? The rest of the group listen in silence. Seek a consensual group decision, but if necessary, accommodate honourable dissenters. Is there a hybrid option that could be reached? Listen to each group's airing of its chosen solution, and ask appropriate questions.

6. **Process Review**. How well did we do, individually and as a group? How could we do even better next time? What are the learning points for us to take as individuals and as a group?

How can I find out more about DBL?

Seminal resource

Dilemma-Based Learning in the Humanities – Integrating social, emotional and thinking skills by Phil Wood, Barry Hymer & Deborah Michel.
Published by Chris Kington Publishing, 2007

This is the only book on DBL available at the time of writing. Its focus is dilemmas in RE, geography and history in the secondary school, but the guidance, Webs and other resources have cross-phase and cross-curricular applications.
Plans are afoot for a primary DBL resource.

The authors can be contacted via email.

Phil Wood: **pbw2@le.ac.uk**

Barry Hymer: **Stillthinkinguk@aol.com**

Deborah Michel: **Debmichel@btinternet.com**

Mystery or
Mastery?

 Motivation –
Intelligence's
Motor

 Grow!

 Relate!

 Act!

 Challenge!

 Exert!

Exert!

Description

'*People of mediocre ability sometimes achieve outstanding success because they don't know when to quit...*' **George Herbert Allen**

The final element in the framework, 'Exert!' suggests that **gifts and talents are created slowly, over time, and usually after much hard work, setbacks and false starts.** In contrast to traditional understandings the E element leads us to expect gift-development to happen irregularly – not linearly – as social, motivational and other conditions change.

Consequently, the E element helps us to understand Jesson's large-scale research which showed that only 28% of children identified as G&T by the end of KS2 went on to get their expected 3 'A' grades at A-level, whereas a significant number of students who were *not* identified as G&T at primary school did.

When faced with such evidence, traditional conceptualisations lead to the blaming of secondary teachers for failing to maintain G&T students' progress, and puzzlement at the 'late bloomers'.

E – a case history

Guess who?

Failed in business	1831
Defeated for legislature	1832
Again failed in business	1833
Elected to legislature	1834
Defeated for Speaker	1838
Defeated for legislature	1840
Defeated for Congress	1843
Elected to Congress	1846
Defeated for Congress	1848
Defeated for Senate	1855
Defeated for vice-president	1858
Defeated for Senate	1858
Elected President of the United States	1860

(Answer: Abraham Lincoln)

Some ways of nurturing E

Here are three ways of nurturing the E element in your classroom:

1. Encourage collaborative group work, and reflections on how the most successful outcomes depend not on the brilliance of the individual members but on ordinary members working brilliantly together. Seek out real-life examples in sport, business (*The Apprentice*), science, etc.

2. Reinforce the slow-burn nature of talent development by introducing your students to the life stories of significant achievers, and the time they took to achieve eminence. Here's one from the comedian Bill Bailey:

   > '22 years I've been doing this comedy lark, so it's been like a meteoric rise to fame ... if the meteor was being dragged by an arthritic donkey across a ploughed field, in Northern Poland'.

3. Get your students to keep portfolios of their work, carefully dated, and periodically ensure they review the progress they're making over time: what can they do now that they couldn't do then?

Implications for whole school policy

Here are four implications of the E element for whole school policy and practices:

1. Prioritise effort, interest and commitment over data when compiling your G&T (or SIG/CEG) cohort. Keep membership fluid, and conditional upon sustained interest and engagement in the activity/programme on offer.
2. Maximise opportunities for the development of collaborative group skills throughout the school and across ages and curricular areas – eg convene 'cabinets of all the talents/interests' to create a school website, prospectus, magazine, school design research groups, a social history project looking at the life histories of past pupils of the school, etc.
3. Find ways of creating and valuing a school 'exo-brain' – a system to harness ideas and suggestions from students, teachers, TAs, admin, catering and grounds staff, to make constant improvements to the school's functioning.
4. Give high-quality PSHE experiences a top priority.

Generating E through LTAR

> *'There is no finish line.'* **Nike Corporation**

Living Theory Action Research (LTAR) consists of a learning journey in which individuals (young and older students, teachers, anyone) ask themselves questions of the sort, *'How can I improve my practice?'*

In responding to such questions over time they seek to resolve contradictions between their values and their practice and in doing so live a fuller, more integrated life. LTAR is, therefore, not really a 'learning tool' at all, nor even an 'approach to learning'. It's the explanations that people generate for their educational influences in their own learning and in the learning of others. Technically, we should talk about 'living theor**ies**' as each account will be unique.

Even more than any other of the 'learning tools' I've already introduced and recommended, living theory action research lends itself to all five elements of the GRACE framework. I've included it in this section because it carries the slow-burn, process-rich nature of enquiry-based learning so strongly and holds sustained, reflexive effort at its very core.

What are the core aims of LTAR?

LTAR doesn't neatly conform to a set of aims and objectives, but part of its rationale is:

- To challenge a traditional social sciences framework of what research and theory might look like
- To offer practitioners (including teachers and students) a robust way of researching and explaining their own practice, and in so doing to produce unique theory (explanations of practice)
- To locate the area of study within the province of the researcher's lived practice (no artificial 'experimental laboratories' are created)
- To harness the researcher's core values as their unique standards of judgment

What does LTAR look like?

An LTAR cycle (or spiral) usually contains the following elements:

You recognise that your educational values are denied in your practice (eg you value critical thinking in your students, but know that you create too few opportunities to develop it)

You imagine a solution to your concern (eg you consider sacrificing some 'content coverage' lessons in favour of P4C sessions)

You act in the direction of your imagined solution (eg you introduce your students to P4C for a trial period)

You recognise that another aspect of your practice isn't congruent with your values, etc.

You modify your practice, plans and ideas (eg you embed P4C more firmly, adapt or improve your practice of it, even ditch P4C for something else, etc)

You evaluate the outcome of the solution (eg you look for evidence that your students are doing more critical thinking)

An LTAR plan of action

For students, as for yourself, the following stages can be helpful in pursuing an LTAR enquiry. The small-scale example is framed within the PSHE domain:

- **What is my concern?** (eg I value all people, yet I treat my younger sister with contempt)

- **Why am I concerned?** (eg I sense that my younger sister is beginning to be frightened of me and to avoid me)

- **What kind of evidence do I produce to show why I am concerned?** (eg I've noticed that she no longer asks to accompany me to town or to come into my room and chat about how things are going. I've begun to reflect on things that I've said to her in the recent past that were hurtful)

- **What can I do about it?** (eg ask her if she'd help me choose a prom dress)

cont'd over →

An LTAR plan of action (cont'd)

- **What will I do about it?** (eg ask her to come with me to town to do this, and thank her generously for her time and advice)
- **What kind of evidence do I produce to show that what I'm doing is having an influence?** (eg she is surprised and delighted to be asked, and at the way I treat her during our shopping trip)
- **How do I evaluate that influence?** (eg see if she tends to take less 'evasive action' when I'm around)
- **How do I ensure that any judgments I make are reasonably fair and accurate?** (eg ask my parents if they sense any change in the relationship my sister and I have with each other)
- **How do I modify my practice in the light of my evaluation?** (eg respond to the feedback from my actions, and act in accordance with the implications)

E for you, through LTAR

Consider the place of the E element as you contemplate using LTAR as a tool for your own educational and personal journeying.

Here's an example of how it might relate to your role as a G&T coordinator or Leading Teacher:

You aspire to a more mastery-oriented approach to giftedness in your classroom/whole school practice

You identify one aspect (however small) that could do with changing/modifying

You implement this change/modification

You reflect thoughtfully on the outcome/s

You generate new insights and understanding

You consider your next steps/actions

And you continue the cycle

How can I find out more about LTAR?

| Seminal resource |

Action Research: Living Theory by Jack Whitehead & Jean McNiff. Published by Sage Publications Ltd, 2006

- ***Action Research for Teachers – A practical guide*** by J. McNiff and J. Whitehead. Published by David Fulton Publishers, 2005
- ***Doing Practitioner Research Differently*** by M. Dadds and S. Hart. Published by Routledge, 2001
- ***Gifts, Talents & Education – A Living Theory Approach*** by B. Hymer, J. Whitehead and M. Huxtable. Published by WileyBlackwell, 2009

Websites with examples of how teachers have embraced LTAR in their own enquiries, include **www.jeanmcniff.com** and **www.actionresearch.net** . Masters degree dissertations you can view at this latter site include:

- *'How does using philosophy and creative thinking enable me to recognise and develop inclusive gifts and talents in my pupils?'* (Ros Hurford)
- *'How do I/we help the students in Key Stage 4 improve their learning if they are in danger of underperforming?'* (Graham Lloyd)

In conclusion – a credo

If you're set on a course of gift-creation in your classroom or school, I'd love to hear from you. You can contact me via Stillthinkinguk@aol.com

Have fun, and good luck!

Quotations for the classroom wall

'Nothing in the world can take the place of persistence. Talent will not: nothing is more common than unrewarded talent... Education will not: the world is full of educated derelicts. Persistence and determination alone are omnipotent. The slogan 'press on' has solved and always will solve the problems of the human race.' **Calvin Coolidge,** politician

'Kites rise highest against the wind, not with it.' **Winston Churchill**, statesman

'In the realm of ideas, everything depends on enthusiasm... in the real world, all rests on perseverance.' **Goethe**, writer

'Let me tell you the secret that has led me to my goal. My strength lies solely in my tenacity.' **Louis Pasteur**, scientist

'Great works are performed not by strength but by perseverance.' **Samuel Johnson**, essayist and critic

'Opportunity is missed by most people because it is dressed in overalls and looks like work.' **Thomas Edison**, inventor

Quotations for the classroom wall

'I'm not like this just because it's a gift. I worked a lot. And this is difficult for everybody – to work.' **Sylvie Guillem**, ballet dancer

'I find that the harder I work, the more luck I seem to have.'
Thomas Jefferson, statesman;
Samuel Goldwyn, movie mogul;
Gary Player, golfer et al

'People always want to know what I'm on. I'm on my bike. Six hours a day. What are you on?' **Lance Armstrong**, cyclist

'I wasn't a very good shot-putter when I started out. By the end of my career it was one of my strongest events.... Through hard work, that's what I did.'
Denise Lewis, athlete

'...you have to do the hard yards and you have to go the extra mile.'
Daley Thompson, athlete

Quotations for the classroom wall

'All great acts of genius began with the same consideration: do not be constrained by your present reality.' **Leonardo da Vinci**, polymath

'Everyone has talent. What is rare is the courage to follow the talent to the dark place where it leads.' **Erica Jong**, novelist and poet

'Satisfaction lies in the effort not the attainment. Full effort is full victory.' **Mahatma Gandhi**

'We must live out our own vision of life. And there will be error. If you avoid error, you do not live.' **Carl Jung**, psychiatrist

'Ever tried? Ever failed? No matter. Try again. Fail again. Fail better.' **Samuel Beckett**, playwright

'I have learned throughout my life as a composer chiefly through my mistakes and pursuits of false assumptions, not by my exposure to founts of wisdom and knowledge.' **Igor Stravinsky**, composer

Quotations for the classroom wall

'The only place where success comes before work is in the dictionary.'
Vidal Sassoon, (amongst others), hairstylist and entrepreneur

'I look out for new, challenging parts. I feel like I'm wasting my time if I repeat myself.' **Heath Ledger**, actor

'It is only because of problems that we grow, mentally and spiritually.'
M. Scott Peck, writer

'It's not the work that's hard, it's us that makes it hard!'

Year 6 pupil, North Tyneside.

'Learning is like circles and spirals. Circles are lazy learning – they go round and round. Spirals is real learning because it goes down and down, deeper and deeper.'

Rory, aged 7, Colne Engaine CE Primary School.

Recommended reading

Classrooms as Learning Communities – What's in it for schools?
by Chris Watkins. Routledge, 2005

The Development of Giftedness and Talent Across the Life Span
by F. Horowitz, D. Matthews and R. Subotnik (eds). American Psychology Association, 2009

Gifts, Talents and Education: A Living Theory Approach
by Barry Hymer, Jack Whitehead and Marie Huxtable. Wiley-Blackwell, 2008

Learning Without Limits
by S. Hart et al. Open University Press, 2004

Mindset – The New Psychology of Success
by Carol Dweck. Random House, 2006

The Routledge International Companion to Gifted Education
by Tom Balchin, Barry Hymer & Dona Matthews (eds). Routledge, 2008

Self Theories – Their Role in Motivation, Personality and Development
by Carol Dweck. Psychology Press, 2000

What's the Point of School?
by Guy Claxton. Oneworld Publications, 2008

Useful resources

100 Intriguing Questions for Kids (Adults too!)
by N Levy. NL Associates, 1994

The Creative Teaching & Learning Toolkit
by Brin Best and Will Thomas. Continuum, 2007

Creative Visualization with Children: A practical guide
by Jennifer Day. Element Books Inc, 2006

The Critical and Creative Thinking Kit
by Jill Swale. Linden Lea Publishers

Don't Just Do Something. Sit There:
Developing Children's Spiritual Awareness
by Mary Stone. Religious and Moral Education Press, 1995

How to Teach Thinking & Learning Skills:
A Practical Programme for the Whole School (ages 5-11)
by Jane Simister. Paul Chapman Educational Publishing, 2007

Little Book of Thunks: 260 Questions to Make Your Brain Go Ouch!
By Ian Gilbert. Crown House Publishing, 2007

Useful resources

Learning & the Brain Pocketbook
by E. Dommett, I. Devonshire & R. Churches. Teachers' Pocketbooks, 2011

Millennium People: The Soul of Success
by Derek Burnett. Hibiscus Books, 2000

Really Raising Standards: Cognitive Intervention and Academic Achievement.
By P. Adey and M. Shayer. Routledge, 1994

Start Thinking: Daily Starters to Inspire Thinking in Primary Classrooms
by Marcelo Staricoff and Alan Rees. Imaginative Minds, 2005

Stories With Holes (a series)
by Nathan Levy. NL Associates

Teaching Thinking Pocketbook
by A. de A'Echevarria and I. Patience. Teachers' Pocketbooks, 2008

A wide range of thinking skills books and resources produced
by Chris Kington Publishers (part of the Electric Word Group)

About the author

Dr Barry Hymer

 Barry is the Osiris professor of psychology in education at the University of Cumbria. He taught in the primary and secondary sectors before training and practising as an educational psychologist and then founding an education consultancy. He is the author or editor of seven books and numerous papers in the fields of gifted education and thinking skills, including the bestselling, radical and influential *Gifted & Talented Pocketbook*. In 2003 Barry received the biennial Award for Excellence in Interpreting Philosophy with Children from ICPIC, the International Council for Philosophical Inquiry with Children.

Acknowledgements: This Pocketbook is dedicated to the many outstanding practitioners with whom I have been privileged to work. Through their tenacity, risk-taking, creativity and clear educational principles they have put theory into brilliant practice – creating new theory in the process – and thereby exemplifying all that is best about educating for gift-creation.

Contact:
Barry can be contacted at: Stillthinkinguk@aol.com or www.barryhymer.co.uk

Order form

Your details

Name _____

Position _____

School _____

Address _____

_____

_____

Telephone _____

Fax _____

E-mail _____

VAT No. (EC only) _____

Your Order Ref _____

Please send me:

Gifted & Talented _____

_____

_____

_____

Order by Post

Teachers' Pocke___

Laurel House, Station Approach
Alresford, Hants. SO24 9JH UK

Order by Phone, Fax or Internet
Telephone: +44 (0)1962 735573
Facsimile: +44 (0)1962 733637
Email: sales@teacherspocketbooks.co.uk
Web: www.teacherspocketbooks.co.uk

Customers in USA should contact:
2427 Bond Street, University Park, IL 60466
Tel: 866 620 6944   Facsimile: 708 534 7803
Email: mp.orders@ware-pak.com
Web: www.teacherspocketbooks.com